MYSTERIOUS
PLACES
of the
WORLD

MYSTERIOUS PLACES
of the
WORLD

RONALD PEARSALL

TODTRI

This book was designed and produced by TODTRI Book Publishers
P.O. Box 572, New York, NY 10116-0572
Fax: (212) 695-6984
e-mail: todtri@mindspring.com

Printed and bound in Singapore

ISBN 1-57717-157-8

Visit us on the web!
www.todtri.com

Author: Ronald Pearsall

Publisher: Robert M. Tod
Editor: Nicolas Wright
Art Directorr: Ron Pickless
Typesetting & DTP: Blanc Verso UK

CONTENTS

INTRODUCTION

The mysterious places of the world retain their awe-inspiring power, even though they have been computer-analysed, subject to archaeologists with the latest tools and techniques at their disposal, carbon-dated, and speculated upon. The theories about Stonehenge alone would, if printed out, would probably weigh heavier than the stones themselves. Yet despite all the expertise we are no nearer to finding the reasons why structures such as Stonehenge were built. This is part of the appeal. One person's theories are as good as the next.

Although world-wide travel has brought many of these sites within reach of almost everyone, they still have the power to overwhelm, even if some of them,

such as Carthage, are becoming the worse for wear, and others, such as Troy, have been "restored" by egocentric archaeologists who thought they knew best. Ancient sites are a ready source of building materials and have often been overlaid by innumerable layers of buildings. Reverence for the past is a phenomenon no more than 300 years old.

What marvels have gone for ever? We are indeed lucky that so many mysterious places have survived and there may be further wonders to uncover. Only recently have the amazing configurations in the Peruvian landscape, viewable only from the air, been known, this vast panorama of abstract shapes without any apparent meaning.

Right: The imposing and spectacular Mayan ruins at Tulum, Yucatan, Mexico.

Previous pages left: The Canyon de Chelly in Montana, United States, is one of the numerous sites in north America reflecting the lives and life styles of indigenous Americans, largely untouched by the invaders from Europe who wreaked havoc in Central and South America.

Previous pages right: Machu Picchu in the Peruvian High Andes, is one of the best-surviving mysterious places, discovered by accident by Hiram Bingham, an American explorer. The site shows the way of life of one of the most out-of-the-way nations of the world, the Incas.

Above: Stonehenge, the best-known of English antiquities, has undergone a whole series of transformations over many centuries, though what it was used for is still a source of mystery, though it probably served some religious or social rite, particularly by the Druids.

Many of the mysterious places are by definition very old. The stone houses of Orkney off the coast of Scotland, the strange cairns and carved stones of Ireland, the Egyptian temples of Abu Simbel, these are no less imposing than a relative "modern", the Taj Mahal in India built 1630-48 by Shah Jehan as a mausoleum for his wife, in which we wonder at the artistry and sheer extravagance rather than anything else.

We are still no nearer to discovering who built many of these places than our ancestors were. The stern statues of Easter Island retain their secrets. Were they erected by people from South America such as the enigmatic Incas? Who created the huge palaces hidden in the depths of the African jungle? What sort of men conceived the Great Wall of China, the only man-made object to be seen from outer space by astronauts?

There is one thing certain . The men who created these masterpieces were every bit as inventive and creative as we are today. The purpose may be hidden from us, but we can fathom their techniques, and "replicas" of Stonehenge have been successfully constructed, though we are still finding it difficult to believe that the original stones were shipped msny miles from Wales

considering the terrain and the absence of roads.

Many of these creations were to the glory of a god, and others such as the Great Pyramid of Cheops are surmised to have been sophisticated astronomical instruments to foretell eclipses or seasonal phenomena with a subsidiary use as tombs. There is a dark side to the picture; in their mountain-top cities the South Americans performed human sacrifices and the multi-deity religions followed by many of the builders are difficult to fathom. Many of the sites in Britain and Ireland, even France, were once held to have been built by the Druids but this theory has been discounted.

The men who erected these often massive structures made it a life-time work, just as did the builders of the cathedrals of the Middle Ages (which would themselves have been mysterious had there been fewer of them!) The quality of the work is often breath-taking, especially in the east, where Angkor Wat, unbelievably still standing despite the long and violent civil war in Cambodia, has sculpture of unparalleled delicacy, obviously the work of love and life-long commitment. Whether anything of the present age will be awarded with the title mysterious must be in some doubt.

Above: The Great Wall of China is the only man-made object that can be seen from the Moon, and considering the primitive tools available its construction is perhaps the most astonishing feat since the building of the Pyramids. But whether it served its purpose in keeping the barbarous hordes at bay is questionable.

Left: The stones of Cornwall are among the most interesting in Britain, of great antiquity, and serving mysterious purposes. The often quaint names - these are known as the Hurlers - have been given them for the purpose of identification. In early times Cornwall was wooded and well populated, and was the centre of a culture of its own which it still strives to preserve.

AMERICA

Mesa Verde

The native Americans had a culture as interesting as that of the first Europeans who arrived in the New World. Or rather they had cultures, for America had a very diverse population, with civilizations in isolated pockets, unable to communicate with others because of the vast distances and inhospitable terrain.

In Colorado, the inhabitants built cliff-side dwellings on the sides of Soda Canyon, now known as Mesa Verde. By the late twelfth century, the Anasazi people had mastered the technique of stone-and-mortar, and built dwellings up to four stories high, with anything from 20

to 2000 rooms. It was an early use of adobe in America, sun-dried brick. The rooms were plastered or white-washed, and sometimes painted. The dwellings were stepped, so that the roof of one building acted as a porch to the one above, and ladders were used for travelling between rooms.

This method was wide-spread, and there are examples in Arizona, including the 19 room Montezuma's Castle, built in a cave 70 feet up of boulders, limestone, and adobe. The Canyon de Chelley has cave-dwellings, including a white-plastered dwelling known as the White House. Cave-dwelling is

Serpent Mound in Ohio, five foot high, 30 feet wide, a quarter of a mile in length, remains a mystery, believed to have been built by the Adenas people. There are other mounds in the shape of animals. The Adenas lived about 1000 AD, and skeletons show that the men were up to seven feet tall and the women six feet. This was a time when most people were smaller than they are today.

These civilizations disappeared as mysteriously as they arrived. It is impossible to say who created the Bighorn Wheel in Wyoming, a giant circle of white stones around a hub with 28 spokes, or what its purpose was. Dating from around 1400, it has been speculated that it was an astronomical device, a popular theory for mystery structures from Stonehenge to the Pyramids.

As in Peru there are also unexplained giant figures laid out on the ground in California, overlooking the town of Blythe, so big that they can be digested only from the air. These include images of men and a horse, radio-carboned at 890 AD before the horse had been introduced by the Spanish and long after the native American horse had disappeared (or had it?)

Above: Cliff dwellings have been used throughout recorded time in all parts of the world.

Previous pages left: Chichen-Itza, Yucatan, Mexico, "The Temple of the Warriors".

Previous pages right: The so-called cliff palace in the Mesa Verde of Colorado.

a widespread phenomenon throughout the world especially in hot climates. They are cool in summer and warm in winter.

Equally remarkable in the United States are the flat-topped earthen mounds, which often towered over villages. There are small ones, possibly for burials, and large ones, probably used for religious and civic reasons, though the purpose of the Great

Chichen Itza

The mysterious places of Europe, Africa, and Asia have a certain family resemblance. Chichen Itza in Mexico is totally different, alien and barbaric, huge in conception and size, with human sacrifice a central feature of the culture. The stepped pyramid, similar to the ziggurats of ancient Babylon, is one of the few buildings that has an echo else-where. The buildings, a curious mixture of square and circular components, are often decorated with semi-abstract relief designs of an obsessional character.

There are extensive remains of Chichen Itza in remarkable condition, especially the menacing statues such as Platform of the Eagles where an eagle is devouring a human heart, and the squat jaguar, a symbol of the

Above: A pyramid detail of Chichen-Itza, Mexico. Although not on the colossal scale of the Egyptian pyramids, the New World examples show high building abilities and the shape remains as a key element in cosmology and religion, often echoed by the pointed or flat-topped mountain such as Fuji Yama in Japan.

Left: Chichen-Itza, Mexico, illustrating the complex and detailed figuration, technically as accomplished as much in the western world.

Opposite: "The Temple of the Warriors", Chichen-Itza, Mexico. The titles assigned to such buildings were purely imaginative, and the purposes of sites in the New World are often mysterious.

Overleaf: "The Temple of Pachamama" (Mother Earth) at Machu Picchu, Peru. The buildings of Machu Picchu were erected to fit in with the natural contours. It belonged to a short-lived epoch, from about 1438 to a century later, when many South American civilizations were destroyed by the Spaniards.

sun in the underground (and therefore night). Among the most eerie sites is the Well of Sacrifice, dredged by an eccentric American, Edward Thompson, from 1904, bringing up human bones as well as gold figures, many of which mysteriously disappeared or which were openly appropriated by his financial backers.

The Maya civilization was sophisticated. It had its own books, on bark or deerskin, written in pictographs, but few survive as most were burned by Christian zealots after the Spanish invasion. Yet it had no knowledge of the wheel, and the arch was unknown. They could not cast metal, and stone tools were used to create the incredible carvings, inscriptions, and statues. However, one of the principle buildings seems to have been an observatory.

Chichen Itza was almost certainly a ceremonial centre rather than a town. It probably dates from AD 423. Additions were made in later centuries when the city was conquered by even more bloodthirsty people, the Toltec

tribe, and many of the existing buildings and sculptures are from the twelfth century. By the time the Spaniards arrived, the city was all but deserted, and was reverting to jungle, though the site was still sacred to the native people.

Machu Picchu

In 1911 or 1912 (accounts differ) the American explorer Hiram Bingham stumbled across a Peruvian city almost completely overgrown in the high Andes 8000 feet (2500 km) above sea level. Excavation revealed it to be in almost perfect condition. The city, or rather town for its population was probably never more than 500, was cunningly built into the towering contours, with buildings shaped to fit the mountain or actually built into it. The stone is granite, and the buildings are mortarless. Outside the city the land is terraced for agriculture, and there are innumerable flights of steps as well as grand buildings and the houses of the peasants who worked the terraces.

Tombs were found containing 100 people of whom 90 were women, giving rise to the theory that they had been sacrificed in some obscure religious rite. The peasant houses had no windows and were grass-thatched, but other buildings, such as the Temple with

Three Windows were more substantial. Pottery was found of some delicacy, but despite its sophistication the Inca culture had not succeeded in making the wheel and the main means of transport was the llama. The building stones were hauled on rollers or on sleds, and stone tools were used to fashion the building blocks.

The Inca civilization had existed in some form since 3000 BC, but it reached its peak in the fifteenth century, and Machu Picchu existed from approximately 1438 for about 100 years, when the Spaniards arrived and

Above: The funeral rock of Machu Picchu. Once completely cut off from the outside world such wonderful sites are now the destination of the intrepid and the venturous.

Opposite: Morning light at Machu Picchu.

destroyed the South American cultures. The city is compact, with a large piazza which served as a market where goods were bartered (money was not in use). As remarkable as the Inca cities were the Inca roads, paved where water would wash them away, which ran the full length of their empire along the Andes, a distance of 3000 miles (4800 km). They were wide, not because they had any transport, but for the quick movement of troops, advantageous for the Spanish invaders, and for royal messengers, who transmitted messages using a code of knots tied in rope. The Incas are among the least known of peoples; elsewhere in Peru is the Mazea Desert with mysterious sand drawings on a gigantic scale, so vast that they can only be interpreted from the air. The present-day Peruvians are equally inscrutable – the women in their bowler hats, the men with large chests and lungs (to be able to survive at high altitude). Were these the people who sailed to Easter Island and erected the stone figures?

Copan

Copan in what is now Honduras was an outpost of the Maya empire, dating from 300 AD to 900 AD and notable for the sheer quantity and quality of the carvings and picturegraphic writings, somewhat obsessional and sinister. It had stepped pyramids – which had been erected since about 500 BC – but unlike the Egyptians for whom pyramids were tombs, Mayan pyramids were topped by temples. Their religion was savage, their gods innumerable and demanding, and human and animal sacrifice was practised. Copan and its surroundings were wealthy as the glass-like mineral obsidian was found nearby, used extensively for cutting instruments and widely traded. Mayan cities were relatively independent, city-states rather than elements of an organised empire.

Copan has an incredible staircase containing the largest quantity of picture writing in Mayan culture. There are few domestic buildings, and it would seem to have been a religious site. The hieroglyphs have not been fully translated; when they have, it would reveal more of an extraordinary era. Where did the Mayans come from? Probably from Mexico and further north about 10,000 BC, though it is probable that we will never know, nor why they were skilled in astronomy – they calculated a lunar month at 29.53020 instead of 29.53059 days – yet had not grasped the usefulness of the wheel (though they had probably worked out the principles).

Opposite: Pyramid ruins at Copan, Mexico. Although the stepped pyramid was the most often-used form in Central and South America, it was also used elsewhere, as in some of the earlier pyramids of Egypt. It is probable that it was easier to build.

EUROPE

Malta

Malta consists of two main islands lying 70 miles (112 km) south of Sicily, and like other Mediterranean islands it took cultures from the mainland and other islands. Unlike Crete and Cyprus, its mysterious places are Neolithic, and are on a colossal scale. More than 30 megalithic temples have been investigated, comprising huge standing stones with horizontal stones between them, hewed from the local stone, limestone. These temples are often in pairs, and the ground plan is often trefoil ("clover-leaf" pattern), implying a sophistication that is indeed rare.

The Ggantija Temples on the smaller island of Gozo stand up to 26 feet (eight metres) high, built about 3500 BC, and is the earliest free-standing building in Europe. Perhaps the best-preserved are the Mnajdra Temples, which resemble a much compressed Stonehenge, with the uprights abutting each other. Malta was settled about 5000 BC by farmers who brought in seed and cattle, and they were probably from Sicily. Some time after 4000 BC the Maltese began to cut chambers in the solid rock for their dead, or they used existing caves, as was the practice in Sicily and along the north Mediterranean coast, but gradually they pursued a wholly new form of archi-

Above: Hagar Qim, Malta, perhaps dating back to the third millenium BC.

Previous pages left: The discovery of Pompeii in 1860 was one of the most important in Europe, sparking off a great interest in antiquity and making archaeology fashionable.

Previous pages right: The temples of Malta are among the most intriguing of mysterious places.

tecture without parallel anywhere else.

During excavations in 1914 at Tarxien on the outskirts of the capital, Valetta, archaeologists discovered the lower half of a huge statue of apparently an earth goddess. These are not uncommon throughout the ancient world and represent squat fat stylised women. Characteristic of the Maltese figures is that an arm is folded beneath the breasts. In the temples are realistic relief sculptures depicting sheep, pigs, and especially bulls, said to be the servants of the earth goddesses, and there

are delicate lyrical carvings representing plants. Some of the temples are large, with interior passages that frequently change direction, with unexplained cubby-holes, perhaps the sanctum of a high priest or priestess.

Analysis of skeletons show that many were light-muscled, not given to physical work such as farming. There certainly was an elite, whether from abroad or developing from earlier farming stock is unknown. The houses of the people have long since disappeared, and as most of the temples are open to the sky there is speculation over what material was used for the roofs.

The building of the temples abruptly ceased about 3000 BC and this curious culture seems to have disappeared 500 years later. New immigrants about 2000 BC found a dead world. The reason for the collapse of this advanced culture will never be known. There could have been a revolt against the priests and priestesses, a natural disaster such as famine, or an invasion, as Malta is uniquely vulnerable not only from Sicily but from north Africa. If this were the case, it would be strange that the invaders did not recycle the thousands of ready-hewn stones for their own purposes.

The world is fortunate that this magical

world was saved by archaeologists early in this century, and that the temples were not casually noted and then built upon or ransacked for building stone as Malta expanded. It is a lesson many civilized nations, such as Britain, could learn.

Troy

For those who imagine Troy as a marvellous capsule in time, with Grecian-style buildings, awesome pillars, perhaps the very gate that admitted the Trojan horse, maybe the odd

Above: An altar found at the temple of Tarxien, Malta, if, indeed, it was an altar, which must remain a matter of doubt, as standing uprights were routinely toppled.

Left: Heinrich Schliemann, the man who discovered Troy in 1870. We will probably never know how much valuable material went through his hands never to be seen again, as he was totally unsupervised and indebted to no one.

statue of Helen of Troy, the reality must be a disappointment, just deep trenches in dusty ground, platforms at various layers, with the most prominent features the high walls and a paved limestone ramp. However, there is no question that it is a mysterious place by virtue of its overtones, one of the most evocative places in Greek myth and legend, though now it is in Turkey.

It is also a salutary lesson in how not to

undertake an excavation. Heinrich Schliemann, born 1822, later a self-made millionaire through trading and smuggling, came to the site of Troy in 1870 and for 20 years he and his crew of 100 workmen dug and dug, uncovering gold, silver, bronze, thousands of artefacts, which he kept hidden from the Turkish officials and so far as possible, with the aid of his wife who was apt to wear the jewellery, from the workmen. There were nine levels, implying nine distinct cities, and evidence of a great fire. Later archaeologists found that there were 46 strata of settlements from about 3000 BC to Roman times. These later archaeologists were more systematic than Schliemann, who died in 1890, and there was so much still to discover (the Pillar House was not discovered until the 1930s).

Considering its vicissitudes – fires, earthquakes, sieges, Asian occupation, massive rebuilding – it is amazing that so much as been done to map out Troy, the higgledy-piggledy houses, the grand buildings – but no temples. It has been speculated that the Trojans had their own personalised religion, which seems dubious.

Emperor Constantine visited the area in 326 AD, did not think much of it, and went a bit further and founded Constantinople (now Istanbul). It will be somewhere visitors can go when they have puzzled over Troy and wonder what it was really like.

Pompeii

In 1834 the English novelist Bulwer-Lytton wrote *The Last Days of Pompeii* but even a best-selling author could not improve on fact. Pompeii is the ultimate time-capsule, buried one fateful day in volcanic ash, which put everything into freeze-frame. It is mysterious, eerie, frightening, elemental, a way of life preserved for eternity. Pompeii is not all complete; most of the roofs collapsed under the weight of the ash, but the people, the animals, the pets, were stifled in mid-breath, their actions caught by a cosmic camera.

It was a modest town of perhaps 20,000 people, surrounded by two miles of wall. Only 60 per cent of the town has been excavated, but four baths, ten temples, two theatres, an amphitheatre,118 bars and brothels, five inns and 20 wine-shops have been located, many of them in pristine condition, with pictures and murals as fresh today as they were on August 24th 79 AD when Mount Vesuvius erupted, or more accurately exploded. The top of the volcano blew off hurling debris into the skies at twice the speed of

Left: A remarkably well preserved statue of Apollo, the Greek god of the sun, standing alone in the ruins of a Pompeii temple.

sound. The "pyroplastic" raced towards the nearby towns at 100 mph. The temperature of the ash was nearly 300 degrees C. The nearby town of Herculaneum had been drowned in boiling mud, though many of the townspeople had managed to escape from there only to fall victim to the choking ash.

The spectacle was seen and recorded by the Roman writer Pliny the Younger (62 AD – c114 AD) (Pliny the Elder, his uncle, had

Left: House of the Deer.

Left: Vesuvius overwhelms Pompeii. Pompeii was only one of the towns to go; Herculaneum was inundated first, watched in horror by the citizens of Pompeii, some of whom had time to escape. Those who avoided the lava flow were killed by the acrid enveloping ash.

35

been unwise enough to take a boat and investigate and consequently died). Herculaneum was discovered by chance by an Austrian prince who was digging for Roman antiquities, and in 1748 an engineer digging in a casual manner discovered a wall painting. Fifteen years later the site was identified as Pompeii, but it was not until 1860 that systematic work was done to uncover the town. It was a sensation. The townspeople were caught as they stood or lay, fossilized for ever in the choking ash.

For the first time it could be seen what a Roman town was really like, and the discovery had a profound effect on architects and interior designers, as well as furniture-makers (Roman furniture was distinctive and sophisticated). The wall paintings were particularly remarkable – the Romans had skills in realistic painting that were not rediscovered until the Rennaissance, and compared with them painters such as Giotto were primitives.

Pompeii was a rich town, peopled by wealthy Romans who had seaside villas there.

It had been a self-governing colony from 80 BC, and was built on a grid-pattern. It was sufficiently modern to have pedestrian crossings on the streets. There were cheap hotels for travelling salesmen and lovers; some have graffiti on the walls. The most moving "artefacts" are the plaster casts made of the dead, now in the museum on the site. If ever there was a place to think of mortality it is Pompeii.

The Cerne Giant

This mysterious figure is a 400-foot-tall naked man holding a club carved into a hillside ten miles from the ancient site known as Maiden Castle, in Dorset, England. The giant's most prominent claim to fame is the erect penis. The turf has been neatly removed to reveal the white chalky subsoil. The Cerne Giant is one of several carvings using this method, the best-known of which is the Abingdon White Horse, in the Vale of the White Horse, Oxfordshire, 374 feet (114 metres) long on a hill 856 feet (285 metres) high. They are stylistically similar, and whereas the giant has a

The bodies of the inhabitants of Pompeii struck down in their daily life without warning and preserved until the discovery of the disaster in 1748.

Left: Forum Street
and Arch of Caligula,
Pompeii.

Above: The Cerne Abbas giant in Dorset, England, now widely believed to be a fraud, but as it is an old fraud it hardly detracts from its appeal.

Opposite: The hand of the Cerne Abbas giant. In close-up, the hand does not look convincing compared with genuine designs of the same type.

"sacred" well the White Horse has a megalith (standing stone) nearby known as Wayland's Smithy. The ancient Ridge Way also runs along the crest of the hill.

It is therefore tempting to think of these carvings as perhaps Iron Age and although the White Horse has been described by archaeological worthies as "unquestionably" prehistoric, there is no such certainty about the Cerne Giant. There does not appear to be a mention of it before 1694, and there is a theory that the owner of Cerne Abbey House, a Member of Parliament and a disillusioned supporter of

Oliver Cromwell, had his servants carve the figure as a satire on Cromwell, who had been mentioned in the annals of the time as the "English Hercules".

The credibility of the Cerne Giant has been tackled by many believers and sceptics. The believers tend to believe that it is a fertility figure, that by his side there was a woman, since covered over (though presumably easy to trace using modern technology), and that the free hand is holding a severed head. The club has also been interpreted as a torch. Some people have claimed that the fig-

Above: As with Carnac, the village of Locmariaquer in western France on the west shore of the Gulf of Morbihan, boasts an impressive collection of very large megalithic monuments. These include the largest standing stone ever discovered. It was once 67 feet high and nine to 13 feet thick but was broken into four pieces when struck by lightning in the 18th century. This particular arrangement of stones is known as the table of the merchants.

figure radiates an unspecific type of energy.

The features of the face are crude, two circles for eyes, arcs for eyebrows, and a slit mouth. These characteristics appear on genuinely old carved stone heads in Cornwall.

The carving of the giant would not have been too onerous as the hillside faces another hill with a similar gradient, and instructions could be yelled across the gap. A group of investigators used this method in constructing a convincing figure of a woman next to the giant using strips of polythene.

Whether it is old or new the Cerne Giant is certainly mysterious, and the very uncertainty about its origins add intrigue to the spectacle.

The Standing Stones of Carnac

Carnac is a small town in Brittany, western France, near the Atlantic coast, population 4243. It is the site of more than 3000 prehistoric stone monuments hewn from locale granite, well worn by time and weather and covered in white lichen. Brittany itself has more in common with Cornwall, and Cornwall has more in common with Wales and Ireland, than the rest of France. All were occupied by Celts. At one time the Celts occupied much of Europe being a fiery warlike people, but were pushed back into the extremities of Britain by first the Romans and then the Anglo-Saxons. Much of Brittany was settled by the people of Cornwall, who brought their own social structures with them and imposed them on the natives. Brittany was largely pagan until the seventeenth century, and only the coming of the railway propelled it into the modern age.

The dolmens or standing stones have parallels in south-west Britain, but not on such a wide scale. They were venerated by the Bretons until fairly recent times, adopted by the Romans for their own religious purposes with Roman deities carved on some of the stones, while the Christians adapted them to their own purposes by fitting them up with crosses and other symbols. The dating of the dolmens (sometimes called menhirs, sometimes cromlechs) is complicated because they were put up at different periods in the Neolithic period, the New Stone Age (8000 – 6000 BC). It was the age when domestication of cattle and systematic farming began, and the settlement of villages was established together with the making of primitive pottery.

Most remarkable of the monuments are the long avenues of stones half a mile (0.8 km) north west of the village, two about a mile (1.6 km) long, one terminating in an

Below: A stark view of the stone avenues north west of Carnac.

Left: Druids in a sacred grove. Druids were once believed to be the builders of Stonehenge, but this theory has long been discarded as they arrived on the scene thousands of years later.

irregular circle after half a mile. The stones vary in size from up to 13 feet to three or four feet as the line proceeds. It has been speculated that the lines were originally much longer, two miles (3.2 km) in length. One line ends in a passage grave covered by a barrow or earth mound, discovered in 1863. A Gallo-Roman villa was discovered by a Scottish antiquary in 1874. Many of the contemporary standing stones in Britain and elsewhere in France (which has the largest standing stone ever discovered – about 67 feet but now broken into pieces) are set in isolation.

The purpose of most standing stones is unknown. Perhaps the lines of stones in Carnac are "pointers", but we can only speculate about what they were pointing at.

Stonehenge

One of the mysteries of Stonehenge, in Wiltshire, England, about which probably more has been written than any other prehis-

Opposite: Stonehenge was built over a long period in three periods, all of which have been scientifically dated. Many of the stones were removed for building purposes, as was traditional with ancient sites, but enough remains to enable us to understand the main design.

toric site, is why so much of it still exists, considering the often cavalier attitude of the English towards ancient monuments. From time immemorial it has been a ready supply of stone to local builders, especially the bluestone brought from the Preseli Mountains in Wales, a distance of 240 miles (385 km), though these were discarded about 2000 BC in stage three of Stonehenge's development. The remains of

Stonehenge are mostly of stage three, a linteled circle within which was a horseshoe formation. The sarsen (greystone) stones were brought from Marlborough downs 20 miles (30 km) away, the nearest source of stone.

Stonehenge was begun about 3100 BC and was a roughly circular ditch; the excavated chalky rubble was used to build a high bank within the circle. Inside this bank a cir-

cle of 56 shallow holes, named the Aubrey Holes after their discovery by the eighteenth-century antiquary John Aubrey. In some of them have been found human remains, put in long after the holes were built. It has been speculated that by covering certain of the holes the makers had a kind of calculator.

Two parallel entry stones were erected on the north-east of the circle, one of which, the so-called Slaughter Stone, remains. This Stonehenge was used for about 500 years and then reverted to scrubland. The second phase involved importing 80 pillars from Wales, weighing up to four tons each, and their transportation remains a poser. The entrance-way of the setting of the bluestones was aligned approximately upon the sunrise at the summer solstice, leading some to suspect that

Above: Stonehenge has parallels throughout western Europe, especially in the British Isles and Brittany, but there is no doubt that Stonehenge, though not the most extensive, is the most impressive.

Above: To this day Druids still regard Stonehenge as place of pilgrimage on crucial days of the year.

Right: Inigo Jones (1573 - 1652) was the most prominent supporter of the Druidic theory of Stonehenge.

Opposite: The Temple of Ceres, Paestum, known as the Basilica, and the Temple of Peace, still preserved well and venerated by the Romans whose cities were built around the temples.

Stonehenge was an astronomical calendar foreseeing eclipses and phases of the moon, or that the inhabitants, if inhabitants there were and it was not merely a religious site, were sun-worshippers.

There are about 600 groups of standing stones in Britain. Who erected them? John Aubrey (1626 – 1697), the first man to look at Stonehenge with anything like curiosity, proposed the Druids. The architect Inigo Jones (1573 – 1652) thought that Stonehenge was built by the Romans. But both the Druids and

the Romans came thousands of years later. The joining of the uprights and lintels of Stonehenge is unusual; mortise and tenon joints were used; the lintels were fitted together using tongue and groove joints, both methods used in carpentry, both methods incredibly rare in architecture, even amongst the master builders.

About 1550 BC holes were dug outside the sarsen circle to put in place the Welsh stones from the earlier period, but this was not carried out and the holes silted up. The blue stones were repositioned inside the existing stones. The largest was given the name the Altar Stone, as it was assumed that the ancients were given to human sacrifice. The sarsen stones are up to 30 feet (nine metres) long and weigh about 50 tons; the surfaces were made smooth by pounding with stone hammers.

Because Stonehenge was virtually unattended until the 1950s, many of the upright stones were toppled and most of the Welsh blue stone uprights have disappeared. Present-day Stonehenge is intriguingly fragmentary, impressive in its wind-swept isolation, though less so with tourist centres et al.

Paestum

Paestum is an ancient Greek city 22 miles south east of Salerno in southern Italy, and is a refreshing example of how cultures can live together. Its glories are the three Doric Greek temples, the Temple of Ceres, the so-called Basilica, and the Temple of Peace, all in a good state of preservation and venerated by the Romans who built their city around the temples. The temples were built over four decades up to about the second century BC. The city was of considerable size with a wall three miles (5 km) in diameter, and although it was sacked by Muslim invaders in AD 871 most of the buildings were left untouched. The city was abandoned, but rediscovered in the eighteenth century, and discoveries are constantly being made, include a Greek fresco of exceptional quality.

Skara Brae

Skara Brae in Orkney, an island to the north of Scotland was uncovered in 1850 when a storm blew away the enveloping sand. In the 1920s archaeologists put the date as about 500 BC, but recent carbon-dating puts the half dozen square round-cornered houses which make up Skara Brae at 3100 – 2480 BC. The houses, in a fine state of preservation, are of stone with no windows, and an earthen floor. Four stone slabs in the centre of the house show where

the hearth was. The beds were stone boxes (not much different to traditional Scottish stone beds) and some of the cooking implements were of whale bone. There were also stone shelf-units, and mysterious boxes let into the floor, perhaps for bait for fishing. The pottery was well-made, and there were stone balls with carved decoration, the purpose of which was unknown. The village itself was built on or in a midden, or rubbish dump, and refuse has been found in several of the houses. It could be that what was rubbish to us was sustenance to them. It all gives a vivid picture of primitive life on a primitive island.

Tara

The mystery of Tara is not what it is, but what it was – the ancient capital of Irish kings. The Irish of ancient times were one of the most sophisticated of ancient races, Celts who occupied much of Europe, warlike, fighting amongst themselves, and ultimately responsible for their own destruction. The standing stones throughout the region are

Above: Tintagel in Cornwall, England, occupies an important place in Arthurian legend. The ruins of the castle are impressive and Tintagel itself has been an important trading place for thousands of years.

Right: The Skara Brae prehistoric settlement in the Orkney Islands off the coast of Scotland is a remarkable site, in exceptional condition considering the harsh weather and showing how life was lived in the distant past when survival was the main object in life.

akin to those found in France, which is not surprising as the early inhabitants of Ireland came from France and perhaps Spain. Tara itself is hardly more than an impressive grassy mound, but in its time it was the scene of unparalleled party-giving and lordly meetings of great ceremony. What gives it a place in history is its aura. Many visitors have sensed it without knowing quite why – perhaps affected by the fairy-folk who were such a feature of Irish myth and legend.

Tintagel

Tintagel in Cornwall, England, is the centre of the King Arthur industry, and a flourishing industry has sprung up catering for those intrigued by the mythology surrounding Arthur and the Round Table. The castle is set at the foot of sensational cliffs, and a good deal remains of the castle, based on a Celtic monastery in use from AD 350 to AD 850. Phoenician pottery has been discovered near the site, giving credence to the belief that the area has much older connections. In 1998 an engraved slate was discovered, mentioning Arthur, but otherwise the relationship between Tintagel and Arthur is somewhat tenuous. Legend claims that he was born here.

Tintagel is rich in atmosphere because of its spectacular setting, added to by the remains of ancient tin mines and slate quarries, and the entire region has a profound air of mystery. The village itself is of great antiquity, and the old post office dates back to the fourteenth century.

Avebury

Avebury in Wiltshire, England, has never been so celebrated as its near neighbour Stonehenge, but its discoverer, John Aubrey, antiquary of the seventeenth century, rated it far more important. A New Stone Age structure, it consists of a circular bank of chalk 1400 feet (425 metres) in diameter, faced by chalk blocks. Within the bank are 100 sandstone pillars up to 50 tons in weight arranged in a circle; this surrounds two smaller circles, and part of a smaller circle. At the centre stood a large stone surrounded by boulders. There is also a U-shaped stone structure, and the Ring Stone, a great stone perforated by a natural hole stood within the main stone circle at the southern entrance. East of the entrance causeway excavations have uncovered a socket for a large timber post.

A route called the Kennet Avenue consists of stones, 80 feet (25 metres) apart,

Left: Tara occupies the most important role in Irish mythology, seat of the ancient kings of Ireland and a vast meeting place for the tribal chiefs. Little is left above ground, as much was probably made of wood, and the Mound of the Hostages passage tomb, again a name invented at some time in the past, is typical of the archaeology found at Tara.

arranged in pairs. This links Avebury with a temple, the Sanctuary, a mile (1.6 km) away. Burial sites were found near four of the Kennet Avenue stones. No-one has explained the purpose of Avebury, and it has not attracted the attention Stonehenge has. Equally mysterious is nearby Silbury Hill, the largest prehistoric mound in Europe. This was never used as a burial site, as mounds of this nature usually were.

It would be idle to pretend that Avebury is as imposing as Stonehenge, but it has a quiet isolated grandeur that places it amongst the great unsolved mysteries of the prehistoric past.

Knossos

Of all the great civilizations of the Mediterranean – the Phoenician, the Egyptian, the Minoan, the Greek and the Roman – the Minoan culture of Crete is the most perplexing and the most intriguing. The

palace at Knossos is the supreme masterwork, begun sometimes between 2000 BC and 1580 BC, levelled by earthquake, and rebuilt. As early as 3000 BC the Minoans (from King Minos the legendary king) had invented their own hieroglyphic script, evolved a sophisticated pottery ahead of its time, and were trading with Egypt.

Knossos evolved piecemeal, and there was no overall design as in Greece, and there is a complex of rooms and passageways, magnificent staircases and store-rooms holding thousands of huge containers for olive oil, lavish halls with breath-taking frescoes. Knossos had a system of sanitation and plumbing without parallel until the Romans, and a religion of their own, with the bull occupying a central place. One of the greatest of ancient legends is that of the Minotaur, half-man half-bull, who lived in the labyrinth in Crete. The labyrinth parallels the twisting and turning of the Knossos passageways.

It was excavated by Arthur Evans in

An interesting 1994 photograph of Avebury with a crop circle. Crop circles were once believed to have uncanny origins, such as the result of space ships landing, but investigations have since exposed them as hoaxes perpetrated by people making patterns in the crops using "ploughs" attached to string fixed to a central post and then revolved, and other similar devices.

1900, and it was found that he had to dig through volcanic ash. Crete was subject to earthquakes (the palace was of brick and wood which was to a degree earthquake-proof), but the volcanic eruption was elsewhere. This event took place in 1450 BC, and the Minoan civilization ceased to exist. It was one of the truly amazing cultures, with a degree of sophistication matched only by Rome and probably considerably more subtle. The vivid frescoes give an insight into everyday life (though some were "restored" by Evans).

The Minoans were sufficiently confident of themselves not to fortify Knossos, and it was clear that Egypt did not present a threat. They traded widely, were expert workers in bronze, their pottery is superb, but they were overtaken by Greece. The civilization eventually declined, never to rise again.

Delphi

It is fortunate that anything remains of Delphi, seat of the most important of all Greek temples, that to Apollo. Delphi was considered to be the centre of the world, the site of the oracle who gave answers to everything and consulted by emperors down, and a centre of Greek myth and legend.

Relentlessly looted – Emperor Nero alone removed 500 statues – a village was eventually built on the site. Its existence is due to the perseverance of French archaeologists who from 1840 began to investigate, though the first major excavations did not occur until 1892.

The French were the most diligent of archaeologists, and though they re-erected some of the fallen pillars, they did not attempt to restore, thinking that they knew best, a besetting sin of many nineteenth-century architects. The village at Delphi was moved wholesale with the financial help of the Greek government, much to the anger of the inhabitants. Built on the steep lower slopes of Mount Parnassus, Delphi had been inhabited since the fourteenth century BC, but the latest temple to Apollo was built in the fourth century BC. Nothing remains of it except the foundation, some steps, and some columns. Many of the stones are left as they were more than a century ago, but there is written evidence as to what Delphi was once like – magnificent. The temple sanctuary was approached by the Sacred Way, lined with "treasuries", where the Greek worthies placed offerings to the gods.

With the coming of Christianity even

Left: The excavation of Knossos was carried out with a good deal of discretion and common sense, unlike Troy. Archaeological excavation was often merely an excuse for wholesale looting, or for rebuilding the site as imagined by the man who discovered it.

Opposite: Knossos is associated with the classical myth of Theseus and the Minotaur, half-man half-bull. The Minotaur lived in an impenetrable labrynth, and had a tribute each year of the flesh of seven youths and seven maidens. It was slaughtered by Theseus who found his way out by following a thread he had laid. The palace itself was labrynthine, so is naturally associated with the legend.

Overleaf: The sanctuary of Athena, Delphi, one of the most revered of ancient Greek sites and sacred to the Oracle, and although less of it is standing than with other archaeological excavations Delphi, in its breath-taking surroundings, has a magic that can hardly be exaggerated.

more effort was made to demote Delphi. It occupied too large a role in pagan religion. There are better-preserved classical ruins, but Delphi has a unique atmosphere and is indeed a sacred spot although its treasures are distributed through the museums of the world. An attempt to rebuild Delphi in the fourth century AD was aborted when the oracle did nothing but wail over the glory that had gone.

AFRICA

Carthage

Carthage, on the north African coast where Tunis now stands, was settled by the greatest trading nation of the ancient world, the Phoenicians, about 832 BC. At its peak it was the only nation in the world which could vie with the Romans and the Greeks, and the conflicts between them spanned hundreds of years. The Carthaginians invaded Sicily with an army of 300,000 (it is said that half of these were captured), and captured Spain. The story of the Carthaginian general Hannibal crossing the Alps using elephants is well known.

Carthage was a great city with one million inhabi-tants. Alas, little is left of its former glory. When building their empire the Romans allowed the conquered to retain a good deal of autonomy, but not with Carthage, so long a threat. It was systematically razed to the ground which was ploughed into furrows and scattered with salt, sym-bolically meaning that old Carthage was dead. The Romans rebuilt it, but their city too was destroyed by the Arabs in AD 698. Eventually the French colonised Tunisia, and during the nineteenth century dozens of archaeologists worked on what was left of ancient Carthage, locating the hippodrome, the forum, and map-ping out the extensive harbour and marvelling at the

Right: The remains of the Roman baths in Carthage.

Previous pages left: Great Zimbabwe, a series of massive conical towers, is one of the wonders of Africa, and for centuries many Europeans refused to believe that such masterworks could be built by the native population, though the high civilizations of Nigeria and other parts of west Africa, long looted by Western explorers and soldiers, should have informed them better.

Previous pages right: Carthage, now mostly hidden under the city of Tunis in north Africa, was one of the few nations that threatened Rome in its prime, and when it was defeated the Romans razed it to the ground and sowed seed so that old Carthage would be gone for ever, though underground tombs remained.

ruins of the Roman aqueduct 56 miles long. The archaeologists, who took away thousands of artefacts, were hampered by the Arab propensity for using ancient ruins as quarries to build their own buildings, and many of the sites were soon covered by modern buildings.

The only traces of the Carthaginians lie in the tombs, which were not found until 1878 as they were deep underground, while others were found by accident after World War I. These contained urns, the contents of which were infants' bones, lending credibility to the histori-

an Diodorus's claim that the Carthaginian religion involved the sacrifice of babies to the god Baal Amon. The French novelist Flaubert wrote a sensationalist novel on this theme.

Had Carthage been elsewhere some of the Roman city may have been preserved, and it may have rivalled its more famous contemporaries, but many archaeologists were more interested in unashamed looting than in, in present day jargon, establishing sites of special scientific interest. If the Pyramids had been a few miles nearer the centre of Cairo,

Above: Hannibal (247 BC - 183 BC) was one of the greatest of ancient generals, and in 218 BC he crossed the Alps with 90,000 foot soldiers, 12,000 horsemen and 37 elephants to conquer Rome. Three-quarters of his men died in the Alps, unused to the hostile climate, but Hannibal still defeated a much larger Roman army.

rather than as they are now near its outskirts, would they have survived, or would the conveniently cut blocks of stone have proved irresistible to builders?

The Pyramids of Egypt

Throughout the history of mankind and its religions, there has been an eager "reaching for the sky", in western Europe by spires, in Islam countries by minarets. In Egypt, Mexico and Peru there are pyramids, of which the Egyptian are the most famous and the most accessible. Unlike some mysterious places, such as Stonehenge, where visitors are sometimes disappointed by the lack of size, the pyramids have a grandeur and a monumen-

tality that more than makes up for the tawdry trappings of tourism. The Great Pyramid of Cheops was the tallest man-made structure in the world until the erection of England's Lincoln Cathedral's Central Tower in 1307. The interior is a network of passages and chambers, broken into periodically by grave robbers and more sympathetically by archae-ologists. It is constructed of 2.3 million stone blocks, some weighing 15 tons.

There are about 80 pyramids and most of them were built between 2700 BC and 2200 BC. Their primary purpose was as tombs, though it has been speculated that they were also astronomical devices, a line of thought common in the present century in respect of

Above: A step pyramid at Sakkara, Egypt.

Left: The imposing
and ever mysterious
pyramids of Giza.

almost any mysterious structure.

The capital of ancient Egypt, Memphis, 14 miles south of Cairo, is long lost except for quite insignificant ruins, especially of the temple of Ptah, and it is evident that the Egyptians regarded functional buildings with indifference. As late as 331 BC when Alexander the Great was appointed pharaoh the population of Memphis was 700,000,

From the earliest times, the Egyptians were a great people in a wasteland of sand – except for the fertile regions abutting the Nile, perhaps the most fertile region in the world. Their preoccupation with death and the afterlife and a complex and a unique cosmology, well illustrated by statuary, wall painting and *The Book of the Dead*, sat side by side with culture and sophistication, a sophistication, exemplified in the Tutankhamun treasures and the elaborate jewellery of the time, some of it made from lapis lazuli from far-off Afghanistan.

There are various kinds of pyramid – the stepped, the "traditional", and there are the Bent Pyramids, in which the upper half becomes more tapered. The population of

Above: Tutankhamun's burial chamber in Luxor. Tutankhamun died young in the fourteenth century BC.

Opposite: The walkway inside the pyramid of Cheops leading to the burial chamber. Many of the Egyptian antiquities have been looted from time immemorial, and have been lost for ever. The finding of the treasures of Tutankhamun in 1922 was therefore an exceptional stroke of luck rather than astute archaeology.

Above: The sphinx had immense spiritual significance to the ancient Egyptians and to much of the world, but an avenue of sphinxes is rare.

Opposite: Exterior of the Temple of Luxor showing fascicled, closed-capital columns forming the courtyard of Amon-Ofis III and Mosque.

Egypt was always large and during the months when the banks of the Nile were under water, the farmers were free to fish, or help, willing or not, construct the pyramids. No doubt black slaves from Upper Egypt (now the Sudan) would have been part of the work force, ferried up the navigable Nile. To the skilled architects, the transport of the stones, by sleds, on rollers, or whatever,

would have presented few problems as there were no great mountain ranges to cross.

The pyramids were surrounded by a complex of buildings, many of which have yet to excavated, including store rooms and shrines. Many of the pyramids have subterranean chambers, perhaps the kingdom of the god Osiris.

Pyramids gave way to obelisks on platforms, serving the same purpose as

pharaohs' tombs, also in groups of imposing buildings. Civil wars, Asian invasions, and the moving of the capital from Memphis to Thebes followed, and only one pyramid was built after 1570 BC. These dates are staggering in their antiquity. It would be another 1500 years before Cleopatra (69 BC – 30 BC) saw them.

Thebes

Thebes, the ancient capital of Egypt, lies 419 miles (675 km) south of Cairo, and is therefore less often visited than the great pyramids, though no Egyptian city has contributed more to our knowledge of early civilizations. Thebes was about six miles square. The main part of the city was on the east bank of the Nile, "the city of the dead" containing the kings' mortuary temples and the houses of his priests, labourers, craftsmen and soldiers on the west. Although part of the modern city of Luxor occupies part of the site, many of the glories of Thebes remain for us to see, not fragmentary ruins, but well-preserved glories from its golden age of from 1530 BC after the capital moved from Memphis.

Great palaces arose, brightly painted and surrounded with gardens, and massive temples were built to the god Amon. About 1111

BC a series of investigations were conducting into the plundering by government officials of the royal tombs in the city of the dead (the necropolis), and the mummies were moved by priests from place to place, some of them to the inaccessible tomb-shaft in Dayr el-Bahri, proving a rich treasure trove to archae-ologists. The temple of Hatshepsut at Dayr al-Bahri was designed about 1473 BC, a series of colonnades and courts on three levels, approached along an avenue of sphinxes, There were galleries, chapels, and the top ter-race contained a hall of columns and a sanc-tuary dug into the solid cliff. The colonnades

Left: Another aspect of
the Colossi of Memnon.

and chapels were richly adored with fine
carvings depicting historical scenes, including
a maritime trading expedition.

The mortuary temple of Amenhotep III
was probably the largest and most splendid of
the temples, unfortunately demolished except
for the foundations, a huge stela (upright

stone slab) 30 feet (nine metres) tall and two
great statues known as the Colossi of
Memnon, now situated like lone forgotten
sentries in cultivated fields, nearly 70 feet (21
metres) tall, each hewn from a single block of
stone. One was known as the "singing
Memnon", because on certain days soon after

Overleaf: The sphinx
and pyramid in Egypt,
perhaps the most pho-
tographed of all the
mysterious places, and
one of the most photo-
genic as the locale can
be approached from
many angles. This
sphinx dates from King
Khafre, of the fourth
dynasty (c 2575 BC –
c 2465 BC).

Above: A further dramatic shot of the sphinx and pyramid at Gaza.

Opposite: Oedipus, later king of Thebes, solved the riddle of the winged Boeotian sphinx, who thereupon killed herself (not slain by Oedipus as modern popularisers maintain), and was one of the most tragic figures in classical legend, unknowingly killing his father and marrying his mother. Thus the Oedipus complex beloved of psycho-analysis.

sunrise it produced a curious high note. Roman tourists including the emperor Hadrian visited it, but when the statue was patched up it sang no more.

Some sites are better preserved than others. Only fragments of a statue of Ramses II exist, but enough remains to calculate that it was 60 feet (18 metres) tall and weighed about 1000 tons. Even when the buildings are incomplete we often see marvellous carvings and reliefs, often of everyday life such as the pharaohs hunting wild cattle in a marshy landscape.

Thebes is ancient history brought to life.

Unlike some Egyptian sites, there was a cult of the living as well as the dead. In 663 BC it was sacked by the Assyrians, and by Cleopatra's time it had been reduced to hardly more than a village visited by tourists especially from Rome. Rome had its own grandeur, and a few hundred years later it shared the same fate.

The Great Sphinx

If the pyramids are awesome, the sphinx adjacent to them is endlessly mysterious. To the ancient world it was a powerful image, a creature with a lion's body and a human head. In

its Greek form it was an oracle. It terrorized people by asking them a riddle: what is it that has one voice and yet becomes four-footed, then two-footed, then three-footed? The answer was man, crawling on all fours when a child, walks on two feet when grown, and leans on a stick in old age. Oedipus – who inadvertently married his mother and then blinded himself and gave his name to the celebrated Freudian complex – answered correctly and the sphinx killed itself by jumping off a mountain.

One of the earliest descriptions of the Great Sphinx was given by Pierre Belon, a Parisian doctor, who after vague speculation described it as having the head of a virgin and the body of a lion. The head, in fact, was that of the ruling monarch, Khafre (c 2575 – 2465 BC) which gives us an approximate date for its construction, though an inscription between the paws states that it represents the sun-god Harmachis. This is not necessarily self-contradictory. The monarchs were given god-like attributes. In certain religious rites, the king as sphinx, makes offerings to deities.

The Great Sphinx, 189 feet long, was built where it was to probably guard the Nile valley. It was known to the Arabs as Abu al-Hawl or the "Father of Terror" Unlike the physically indestructible pyramids, it has worn less well, especially the face, but this deterioration seems to have been fairly recent as eighteenth-century engravings and drawings show convincing detail now lost.

The cult of the sphinx moved to Assyria (now Iraq) and then to Persia. The Assyrian sphinx had a bearded face, but a characteristic of Asian sphinxes is that they had wings. The sphinx reached Greece about 1600 BC, and often wore a flat cap with flame-like projections. Later Greek sphinxes were almost always female, often had long-tiered wigs, and the wings became more elegant and flowing. They were often used as decorations on vases, ivories, and metal, going out of favour about 1200 BC and reappearing 400 years later. They were also used in temples, where, as in Egypt, they seem to have had a protective role.

Throughout modern history sphinxes have reappeared as decorative items on furniture, especially after Napoleon's experts diligently recorded Egyptian antiquities, and there was a vogue for sphinxes in the 1920s with the revival of interest in all things Egyptian following the Tutankhamun excavations. By this time the sphinx had lost its menace; it was now hardly more than "amusing".

Opposite: Temple of Amon seen from the sacred lake, Karnak, the village of central Egypt which occupied part of the site of the ancient city of Thebes,

Karnak

Karnak comprises the northern ruins of Thebes, and dates back to about 3200 BC, more than 1000 years before Thebes was made capital of the pharaohs. The most northerly temple is the Temple of Mont, the war god, but only the foundations survive. The glory of Karnak is the temple of the state god, Amon, but this is not one temple but a complex of temples, one of the largest in the world, added to and altered through the centuries so that there is no coherent plan. There are no fewer that ten "pylons" (temple gateways) separated by courts and halls. Lavishly decorated with strange animals and plants brought back from Asia, the temple has been described as a great historical document depicting the rise and fall of the Egyptian culture.

The most striking feature of the temple is the pillared hall begun about 1307 BC, 5800 square yards (4850 square metres), with 14 columns 78 feet (24 metres) high. Seven aisles at the side bring the number of columns up to 140. On the outer walls are historical reliefs depicting battle scenes. Karnak presents a great problem to the dedicated architects who seek to preserve it, as the Nile's annual flood has disintegrated the sandstone at the base of walls and columns. Constant repair and strengthening has meant that hundreds of new discoveries have been made in recent years, including evidence of the conflicts between supporters of the god Amon and supporters of the god Aton, during which time temples of the rival god were destroyed or modified.

In other temples, such as the so-called festival temple, the columns taper downwards, a strange feature which was soon discarded, but it illustrates the delight the Egyptian architects had in experimentation, and their skill in making such an oddity work. In most of the temples, the general public had no part to play; they were reserved for the priests and the chief priest, the pharaoh, though there was one temple where the people were encouraged to make supplications to the god. The god was supposed to lean towards the person making the request.

It is doubtful whether Karnak will ever been fully excavated, for eventually the waters of the Nile will surely win the battle.

Abu Simbel

In the ancient civilizations, the edges of the empires were always vulnerable In the south of Egypt were the Nubians, with whom the pharaohs were frequently in conflict, though the outcome of any conflict was never in

Opposite: The so-called hypostyle ("having the roof supported by pillars") hall of Karnak. Karnak was the largest temple in Egypt, more accurately a complex of temples, and one of the largest in the world.

doubt, unlike the threats from Asia. In the extreme south of Egypt, at Abu Simbel on the west bank of the Nile, Rameses II (sometimes spelled Ramses) built a pair of temples. He reigned 1279 – 1213 BC, was one of the great pharaohs, and he knew it. Thus the main temple is fronted by four huge statues of Rameses II, two on either side of the entrance. The statues are 67 feet (20 metres) tall, seated with the hands on the knees, and near the feet are members of his family, and images of gods.

The most remarkable thing about the temples is that they are carved into a sandstone cliff, and were unknown to the outside world until their rediscovery in 1813. They were first explored four years later by an early Egyptologist, Giovanni Battista Belzoni. Despite the site being so deeply inland, it was still relatively fertile, though wells had to be drilled to supply water.

The main temple consists of three

consecutive halls extending 185 feet (56 metres) into the cliff, decorated with a variety of figures and painted reliefs illustrating Ramses' successful wars and domestic scenes, including oryx and other wild beasts wearing collars, and it is believed that Ramses was one of the first people in the world to have a zoo. The first hall contains eight massive pillars, each having a likeness of Ramses, and the temple was so built that on certain days of the years the first rays of the morning sun penetrated its entire length and lit up the shrine in the furthermost sanctuary.

To the north of the main temple was a smaller one, dedicated to Ramses' wife Nefertari, with 35 foot statues of the pharaoh and his queen.

There were less substantial rock temples along suitable stretches of the Nile where there were sandstone cliffs, but Abu Simbel has a special claim to fame in that it was nearly doomed, being in the way of the Aswan High Dam built in the 1960s. However, instead of being casually inundated, the fate of many ancient sites, the temples were completely disassembled by digging away the top of the cliff and reconstructing them on higher ground, a tribute to UNESCO, the much-maligned Egyptian government of President Nasser, funds supplied by more than 50 countries and the innovative technology of the period. Although sandstone is easy to cut, it is easy to damage. A concrete dome was built over the temples to take the weight of an artificial earth mound. Let us hope that the lesson of conservation is taken on board when, as is inevitable, future early sites are threatened.

ASIA & THE PACIFIC

Angkor Wat

Angkor Wat is the largest religious building ever built. Deep in Cambodia (Kampuchea), it was discovered overgrown, deserted, but amazingly complete in 1860 by a French naturalist Henri Mouhot. The region, not named Indo-China for nothing, was a melting pot of Chinese and Indian influences, though Angkor Wat is Hindu in conception. The Khmer kingdom, made notorious by the Khmer Rouge, came together about 600 AD. Angkor Wat dates from between 1113-1150, contemporary with the great cathedrals of Europe, and they have something in common – intricate even obsessive decoration, scale, and sublime and anonymous architectural skills.

The European cathedrals were places to worship. Angkor Wat was the spiritual home of the Khmer gods, and there are five "temple-mountains" on its summit, echoing the sacred Mount Meru of the Hindu religion. The ground plan of the temples is square, but becomes star-shaped as it ascends. Despite the tremendous weight, there are no prepared foundations. Surrounding the temples are walls, galleries, arcades, and self-contained pillared buildings, all surrounded by a moat 650 feet (200 metres) across.

Previous pages left: One of the Buddhist temples in the Angkor Wat complex in Cambodia, once in the total grip of the jungle and which always threatens to over-whelm the largest reli-gious site in the world.

Previous pages right: Temple at the Ellora caves north east of Bombay in India, a three-stories high building cut out of solid volcanic rock in the eighth and ninth century.

Angkor Wat itself is not isolated, and there are other temples throughout Angkor – Bayon is as amazing, a forest of 54 towers around a central edifice with giant Buddha-like faces smiling from the sides of the towers. Angkor was one of the largest cities in the world and of all the mysterious places in the world Angkor Wat may take pride of place as the most awesome. The sculptures, carvings, and bas reliefs are not focused as in the Christian religion, and not only tell the stories from the great Hindu sagas the Mahabarata and the Ramayana but contain astonishingly realistic bas relief carvings of everyday life. These sculptors conveyed figures in motion, as exact as the ballet dancers in Degas' paintings and drawings, a phenomenal achievement and far more sophisticated than anything happening in the west.

There are strange gods, curious animals, the god Vishnu with three eyes, the voluptuous naked maidens so familiar in Indian sculpture and architecture, as well as Buddhist elements. They are piled on in abundance, whether or not they can be seen by the visitor. The entrance, through a massive gateway, is so aligned that the five towers are seen to their best advantage. When Mouhot discovered Angkor Wat he asked

the local population if they knew anything about it, and was told that it was the work of giants. All recollections of the great civilization had gone, for it was sacked in 1431. The rulers had been so intent on constructing their huge temple-mountains that they had neglected the first principles of survival.

It is a story echoed throughout the world. Parallels can be drawn with the Inca

and Aztec civilizations, though more is known of the Khmer rule thanks to visitors from China, who wrote of the Khmer ability to construct reservoirs and canals, their aversion to trade with other countries as they were self sufficient, and the important role of women in administration as well as everyday life. Visitors also noted the Khmer propensity for warfare at the least provocation.

Ur

Ur was one of the principal cities in "the cradle of civilization" Mesopotamia, now called Iraq, and was first systematically excavated in 1854. Its main feature was its ziggurat ("stage-towers"), a massive stepped pyramid, built about 2000 BC, which when it was first located was a mysterious ruin. More is known of Ur than most ancient sites, because the

The main temple of Angkor Wat, portraying the immense detail and convolutions so typical of Hindu and similar religious buildings.

quantity of material excavated has rarely been equalled, and their writing – the first literature – was deciphered in the nineteenth century. Ur was sacred to the moon-god Nannar, sometimes known as Sin, and is said to be the birthplace of Abraham.

The great archaeologist of Ur was Sir Leonard Woolley, who started work there in 1922 – the year when Tutankhamun's tomb was discovered – and carried on until 1934. There were many layers to uncover, and it was found that a great city had been there since at least 4500 BC and was inhabited until 500 BC. It was believed by many to be among the oldest of cities, but it has been proved that Jericho dates back to at least 7500 BC. Ur was a major trading centre, situated at the junction of the rivers Euphrates and Tigris. Woolley traced the boundaries of the ancient city, uncovered areas of ordinary housing, several palaces, groups of royal tombs, and two harbours.

With rare exceptions, such as in some of the tombs, the building material was brick. There was no local stone and no timber, except that imported, especially cedar from Lebanon. Bitumen was used as a setting for the brickwork, but the foundations were never firm, and the ziggurat was rebuilt several times. Ur was not the largest of the cities. At its peak it could have contained 20,000 people and it covered 450 hectares (148 acres), only a seventh of the size of a lesser-known city, Uruk.

During his excavations Woolley found evidence of the Biblical flood (a ten-feet thick layer of mud), and this was backed up by bas relief carvings found elsewhere. He sent a telegram to England – "We have found the Flood". The written tablets showed that Ur imported all kinds of metals including copper, silver, and gold, soapstone from Iran, and cotton, and it exported textiles, pottery, art works of all kinds and especially items of metal, in the working of which the inhabitants were highly skilled.

The most marvellous objects came from the royal tombs, but there were so many ordinary tombs in what was known as the "Death Pit" that it was apparent that Ur was not only a centre of trade but a centre of burial. When a king died, all the mourners were also put to death by priests apparently by poison. There is no evidence that they objected to this. Grave robbers had, of course, been busy, and it is remarkable that Woolley managed to find so many art objects and artefacts. Many of them lay close to the surface, and they continue to appear, sometimes by accident.

Visitors to Ur will be surprised and misled by the pristine condition of the ziggurat. It has been partially but lavishly reconstructed in this century. The carrying out of such work is to many archaeologists reprehensible, but it does enable strangers to get some idea of the grandeur of this ancient civilization. Babylon lies 140 miles away, but it has yielded little, and although there was evidence in the nineteenth century of the Hanging Gardens this has largely disappeared.

Left: The Persians were one of the great civilizations of the past, and Persepolis echoes the grandeur of the time. One of the most important kings was Cyrus, who ruled from 550 - 529 BC and was master of Asia from the Mediterranean to the Hindu Kush, a religious conciliator when these were few and far between.

Left: Alexander the Great (356 - 323 BC) of Macedon, the conqueror of the Persians when he was only 22, and who in a debauched state after conquering half the known world laid waste to Persepolis. He also conquered India when it was but a name. His name lives on in the Egyptian metropolis of Alexandria, and he was responsible for the wide diffusion of Greek ideas and civilization,

Persepolis

The great citadel of Persepolis was built by Darius, king of Persia, from 520 BC onwards and it was never finished. Even the masons' rubble was left on site. It was sited in bleak inhospitable country with sparse rainfall, and it was a prestige complex used for ceremonial purposes and perhaps holidays for the king, his queen, and the court. The audience hall, probably took 30 years to construct and had 72 mighty pillars, only 13 of which remain standing. The throne hall had 100 columns, and was the largest building. There was also a treasury, cramped soldiers' quarters, and a harem. The buildings and walls are rich in bas reliefs and carvings, often distinctly Egyptian, probably because a large number of Egyptian workers were used. These carvings are sometimes monumental, sometimes quietly domestic.

There were no temples. The court religion was Zoroasterianism. Zoroaster was a religious teacher and prophet who lived shortly before Persepolis was built, and it was an "abstract" religion without a multitude of deities, so remote from the ordinary people that it eventually lapsed. Religion was an individual matter governed by personal morality and the struggle of good against evil. It was a religion for sophisticates, which the Persians assuredly were – fair-skinned Aryans from the steppes of the north (the present-day word for Persia, Iran, derives from Aryan). The Persian Empire was the most powerful in the world, and probably the most benign. The conquered countries, such as Egypt, were given almost complete autonomy. It is difficult to say how far the empire extended, but Carthage in modern Tunis was regarded as a vassal state.

The key to the Persian success lay in three remarkable rulers, Cyrus, Darius and Xerxes, and in the army. The army, unencumbered by armour, was based around skilled bowmen and cavalry. They carried all before them until they came up against the Greeks at Marathon where it suffered defeat (though the Greeks could not win back the Persian territories of Egypt and Cyprus).

Far from other existing buildings, Persepolis is one of the most isolated of all the mysterious places. Until a hundred years ago, it was little known, and was noted only for its magnificent double staircase and the enigmatic ruins of buildings built of dark-grey marble from the surrounding mountains, and the huge pillars. Its renaissance is due to two twentieth-century shahs of Persia who systematically excavated it and restored it.

The Greeks themselves knew nothing of Persepolis (which they named) until it was taken by Alexander the Great in 331 BC. In revenge against the Persian burning of Athens, Alexander retaliated and destroyed it, taking back with him gold and silver bullion on the backs of 3000 pack animals. Much of the Persepolis legend was written by the Greeks who were not altogether reliable, and Persepolis continued to be the capital of Persia for some time, whatever Alexander had done to it.

Taj Mahal

The Taj Mahal is not mysterious because of its antiquity – it is the most modern of the places in this book – but because of its magical perfection, undimmed by the 350 years between its erection and today. It was begun in 1632, and a work-force of 20,000 was employed, including Venetian jewellers and French gold-smiths. No expense was spared and the original main gate was made of solid silver.

The centrepiece, the mausoleum itself, was completed in 1643 and the whole complex including mosques, the gateway, and the wall took 22 years to complete. It was built to commemorate the Mogul emperor Shah Jahan's wife Mumtez Mahel who died in 1631 giving birth to the couple's 14th child. It is predominantly of white marble, but many other materials were used including red sandstone.

The complex consists of a rectangular area 1902 by 1002 feet (580 by 305 metres) and is aligned north and south. It is perfectly symmetrical; in the centre is a square garden area, and the mausoleum is flanked on either side by two identical buildings, a mosque and its jawab, a term for a purely decorative building to act as a balance for the mosque. A high boundary wall with octagonal turrets at the corners surrounds the northern section and the central garden, with four square lawns, each divided into 16 give 64 formalised flower beds.

It was not a place of solemn quiet, and the gardens would have been frequented by peacocks and other exotic birds. They were also used by court officials for picnics. To protect the tame birds and the flower beds there were guards equipped with peashooters to keep off predatory birds. The Taj Mahal is reflected in an expanse of water, and the whole place is rich in symbolism, though, unlike the places of antiquity, there are no images of humans, this being forbidden by the religion, and the decorative elements are supplied by geometrical and abstract inserts

Left: The Taj Mahal, Agra, in India, a monument to architectural perfection and preserved in pristine condition, a truly magnificent edifice for a prince and his wife.

and by sacred text set into the stone in contrasting colours.

The mausoleum itself stands on a marble plinth 23 feet (seven metres) high, and has four identical facades with chamfered corners and a massive arch that rises to 108 feet (33 m) on each face. The double dome is bulbous and is supported by a tall drum. The skyline image is created by parapets over each arch and by pinnacles and domed kiosks over each corner. A three-stored minaret stands at each corner of the plinth, with marble bricks contrasting with the highly finished pure marble of the mausoleum. All is perfection.

Shah Jahan had intended to have an associated mausoleum in black marble for himself, but did not live to see this project and he is buried here with his wife. The tombs are decorated with contrasting stone and enclosed by a perforated marble screen studded with precious stones. Unlike most buildings, it has not been altered or interfered with in any way, as this was contrary to Mogul building practice, and the Taj Mahal is as fresh today as it was then. It can be seen as a supreme work of art rather than a piece of architecture and encapsulates an era of studied magnificence.

Yoshinogari

The Yayoi culture (c250BC – AD 250) was an early culture of Japan, named after a district in Tokyo where its artefacts were first discovered in 1884. It arose on the southern island of Kyushu and gradually spread northwards. The Yayoi people mastered iron and bronze casting, wove hemp, lived in guarded communities of thatched-roof raised-floor houses and cultivated rice, millet, melons and gourds. and they produced unglazed pottery, preparing the clay in the shape of ropes and coiling it spirally upwards, incising it with abstract designs, and finishing it in red.

The Yayoi people lived in communities, one of the best known being Yoshinogari, surrounded by a moat 3000 feet (650 metres) long. As it was an unsettled period guard towers studded the periphery of the site. Although the buildings have long disappeared we know about them from a book Wei Chih completed in AD 297. As with many old cultures, there was a preoccupation with funerals and death and the site of Yoshinogari is rich in tombs and graves, and their contents. There are several thousand urn graves, 350 cave graves, and some stone box graves, and it is the most remarkable burial site in Japan. The skeletons themselves are often headless,

Opposite: Unquestionably the Taj Mahal, one of the best-known great buildings in the world, if not the best known, has always had the power to awe and overwhelm, and has influenced the design of many buildings the world over, often in a weird and off-beat form such as the Brighton Pavilion on the south coast of England.

Overleaf: The Palace and Corinthian tombs of the cave city of Petra, Jordan, carved out of the red rock. "The rose-red city half as old as time" was not known until 312 BC, was occupied by the Romans, then the Moslems. Later it became a Crusader outpost before falling into oblivion. Petra was rediscovered in 1812 by a Swiss travellers.

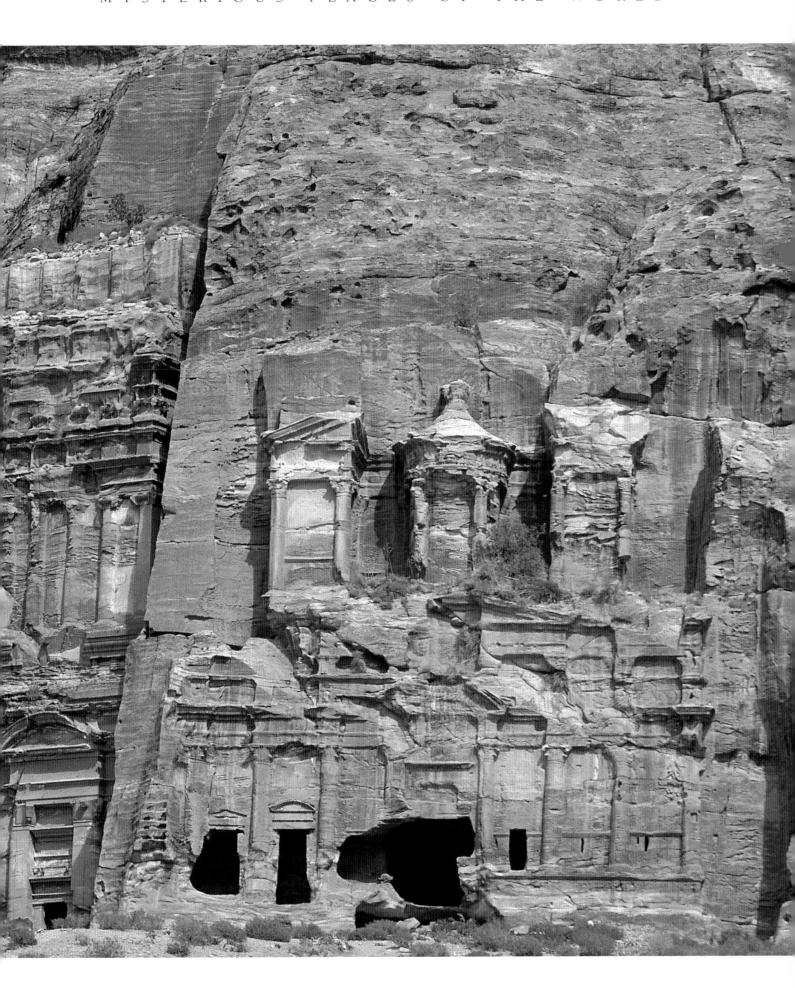

sometimes are pierced with arrows, and all speak of conflict and warfare. The dead vary in status, and were often buried with belongings, such as bronze mirrors and weapons. At the northern end of the settlement is a large burial mound, constructed using alternate layers of red and black earth, and erected on a large octagonal platform.

Although the Yayoi culture spread northwards, it was relatively unsophisticated and essentially agricultural. What is remarkable is that Yoshinogari was discovered at all as the Japanese have an aversion to prying with ancestral remains, and this accounts for the relatively untouched relics of the past as grave robbers would have been as inhibited as their law-abiding contemporaries.

Petra

Petra "the rose-red city half as old as time", is in Jordan and is remarkable for its rock-cut buildings with their elaborate facades. The local material is sandstone veined with red and purple varying to pale yellow, and the buildings, in the centre of an Arab kingdom, are remarkable for their restraint and beauty, more Hellenistic than most sites in the area. Up to about 312 BC little was known of Petra when it was a centre of the spice trade and on

an important trading route, but the Romans occupied it in AD 106. A severe earthquake damaged the city in AD 551, Islam invaded in the seventh century, and there was a Crusader outpost there in the twelfth century. Petra was then long lost until rediscovered by a Swiss traveller in 1812. The celebrated rose-red buildings were tombs, but "The Monastery" dating from the third century AD was used in Byzantine times when the area was Christian as a church. Other buildings were used as dwellings. Because of its isolation, Petra has always had an aura of mystery.

The Great Wall of China

The Great Wall of China is the only man-made object that can be seen from the Moon. Stretching 1500 miles (2400 kilometres), it was begun about 214 BC. It is 30 feet (nine metres) high, and 15 feet (four and a half metres) broad at the top, and although it was extensively rebuilt in the fifteenth and sixteenth century it must be regarded as a monumental achievement that has stood the test of time. It snakes through valleys and hills, with thousands of watch towers which were large enough to store large quantities of provisions of a siege. The building materials vary depending on what local stone was available.

Opposite: A view through one of the turrets placed at intervals along the Great Wall of China.

Left: First built about 300 BC, the Great Wall of China encompasses a distance of 2400 km (1500 m). It does not cover the entire northern border of modern China.

It was built to keep out the marauding hordes of the north, and the wall was still used for this purpose as late as the Ming dynasty (1368 – 1644), though its purpose was to keep China in as a self-contained country as much as to keep predators out.

The Forbidden City of Peking

The capital of China has varied over the millennia, and Peking was first established as capital in the Yuan period (1260 – 1368 AD), though the capital later moved to Nanking and back again, being firmly established in the Ming dynasty (1368 – 1644). The Ming dynasty was highly cultivated, rich in tradition, and lavish in ceremonial. The emperor was all-powerful, and the Forbidden City was conceived, with administrative buildings, accommodation for several wives and their children, and temples. This was a city within a city; there was the Chinese city, the Imperial city, and, in the outskirts, the Tartar city.

The Forbidden City was surrounded by a broad moat, and built according to the rules of feng shui, in which alignment and interior design were vitally important. An astrologer was consulted alongside architects. It was a custom-built city, and most of the buildings are lavishly adorned but low, often single-sto-

Left: The Forbidden City of Beijing can be seen as series of Chinese boxes, a city within a city within a city, with its own incredible logic.

ried, though taller buildings would have been unstable because of the widespread use of wood. One of the tallest buildings is the main gate, closed at sunset, but there were several gates before reaching the imperial palaces, the centre of the complex. Practicality vies with spirituality; the Dragon Pavement of inset marble was only used by the spirits, and never even by the emperor.

The centre piece of the palace were three great ornate halls, the Hall of Supreme Harmony, the Hall of Perfect Harmony, and the Hall of the Preservation of Harmony, all of which had their specialised functions conducted with elaborate ritual, though perhaps the most attractive feature of the palace was the imperial garden with exotic trees and perfumed by vast incense burners.

110

of the sites have been built upon or plundered for building materials, the ancient capital of Sri Lanka, Anuradhapura, has been preserved as an "archaeological park", with its overtones of Disneyland. Nothing could be further from the truth. The old city of Anuradhapura is the best known of early Sri Lanka sites, with its huge bell-shaped dagobas (Buddhist commemorative shrines) built of small sun-dried bricks, temples, palaces, sculptures. A characteristic of Sri Lanka buildings is the pair of gigantic animal feet which flank the entrances of the major edifices.

Anuradhapura, a modest town of about 37,000 inhabitants, was the capital from the

Above: A temple in the Forbidden City, Beijing. Despite the upheavals during the Great Leap Forward the Forbidden City somehow managed to remain sacrosanct.

The Forbidden City remained inviolate for centuries until the arrival of the Europeans after the Boxer Rebellion of 1900, who had their own ideas of ceremony, largely looting, raping, and burning.

Anuradhapura

Sri Lanka shares much of its archaeological legacy with India. But whereas in India many

Left: It will probably never be known who carved the unique statues of Easter Island, whether they were voyagers from South America or from south-east Asia.

fourth century BC to the eleventh century AD, when invasions from India resulted in a change of capital, and it was abandoned and reverted to jungle. It was discovered by the British in the nineteenth century and became a Buddhist place of pilgrimage as the city contains an old pipal tree (bo-tree), believed to be a branch of the tree under which Buddha sat. The branch was planted about 245 BC and is believed to be the oldest tree in the world of which there is any historical evidence.

Easter Island

Easter Island lies 1400 miles east of Pitcairn Island (where the mutineers from The Bounty were stranded) and 2000 miles west of Chile, the ruling power. It was perhaps discovered by a man named Davis in 1686 who named it after himself. It was given the name of Easter Island because it was discovered on Easter Day itself in 1772 by Admiral Roggeveen. Captain Cook rediscovered the island in 1774. He called it Teapi or alternatively Waihu, though its real name is Rapunui.

The Spanish came and persuaded the natives to sign the island over to them although nothing was heard from them again. The most benevolent visitor was the Frenchman, Comte de la Perousse. He

brought with him seeds, sheep, goats and pigs. The animals were intended for breeding but were eaten by the islanders instead.

Discoverers faced a curious civilization in terminal decline. All were immediately in awe of the 600 giant statues of long heads and stylized torsos facing inland, usually about 16 feet high, though some were larger and some smaller. Those which were not toppled at the

Above: The great English explorer James Cook (1728 - 1779) did more than any navigator in discovering the islands and countries of the Pacific

Opposite: An Easter Island statue with eyes of inlaid sea-shell. Many of the statues had fallen over the centuries but many have now been re-erected.

Left: Restored stone statues on Easter Island (known as moai) standing on the original platform. The hat or wig-stone is clearly seen.

Right: Although it had long been thought possible that rafts and simple boats could make the journey from South America to the central Pacific islands it was not graphically proved until the Norwegian ethnologist, Thor Heyerdahl, did so soon after World War II. Heyerdahl also crossed the Atlantic in a papyrus boat, a feat less generally known.

time eventually suffered the same fate later. A curious feature of the statues was that they all wore block-shaped hats carved from a distinctive red rock.

As remarkable as the statues were the 300 large stone-studded platforms, some of which were more than 100 feet long. The earliest of these was carbon dated from 700AD. They are generally built on headlands facing the sea. The stones used were close fitting and had no cement to bind them together. Houses on the island were constructed in the same way.

The material from which all except the earliest of the statues was carved was from volcanic stone (there are three extinct volcanoes on the small 45 mile square island). This stone is soft when quarried and very hard when exposed to air.

The reason the statues were built is most unusal. There were ten clans or tribes on the island and they all vied with each other in their respect for the dead. A funeral could last for years.

The "living faces" were tokens of esteem for the ancestors of the islanders. In around 1680 the natives stopped making them, abandoning half-built figures in the quarry, including one 65 feet tall. They then turned their attention to carving and engraving "birdmen"

in the stone. The Birdman was the chief of the clan leaders for a year, following a race to bring back a tern egg.

The Easter islanders developed their own pictographic language, inscribed on wooden boards. These were later used as firewood. But where did they come from? No-one really knows. Some think they came from beyond Polynesia in the west. Thor Heyerdahl, intrigues by local legend, made the voyage from South America on a Peruvian-style raft called the *Kon-Tiki*.

Easter Island is remote from other Pacific cultures; it is speculated that one wave of immigrants arrived between 400AD and 500AD; another around 1200, with little outside influence after that. By the time the Europeans arrived, the land was deforested, civil war raged and canibalism prevailed.

At its peak the population was around 10,000. The discoverers found only 2000. This was reduced even further when many of the islanders - probably half the total poplulation - were captured by the Peruvians to work their guano (bird droppings used for manure) farms from 1859 onwards.

The Peruvians were persuaded by the Catholic church to take the islanders home

but many died in transit and from various diseases including smallpox. This brought the population down to scarcely more than 100!

Later, Christian missionaries arrived, converted the islanders and restored self-belief. Traders fron Tahiti introduced cattle and sheep commercially.

Ayers Rock

Today there are up to 2000 people living on Easter Island, supported by modest agriculture, fishing and some tourism.

And the mysterious stone figures are now once again mounted on their platforms, restored by the Chilean government for all to see and marvel at.

Ayers Rock is undoubtedly Australia's most impressive natural feature. Looming out of the central plain it completely dominates the entire area and can be seen from 60 miles away.. There are no foothills and the rock veers straight upward to a height

Below: A dramatic portrayal of Ayer's Rock, Australia, at dawn. Although a natural feature, Ayer's Rock is of very great religious significance to the native Australians, or Aborigines.

Previous page: Because of its extreme isolation in the arid outback, Ayer's Rock was for a long time little known to outside travellers. It appears awesome as well as mysterious.

of 1143 feet.It is a bleak, barren place though none the less starkly beautiful. The rock supports no life whatsoever, not so much as a bush or a blade of grass.

The native Austalians, known as Aborigines, hold the rock a most sacred place, believing it to be the home of their ancestral gods. The walls of the larger caves at the base of the cliffs are covered with ancient Aboriginal decorations, mostly in homage to their deities.

Left: Along with the Great Barrier Reef, Ayer's Rock is one of the grandest natural glories of Australia.

Ayers Rock has a circumference of almost six miles and is thought to be around 450 million years old, the last surviving remnant of a much larger mountain chain, formed by the earth's shifting plates. It is made from sandstone and is so vast that it almost creates its own weather system. The rock also changes colour - from terra cotta at dawn, mauve during the day and a fiery red at sunset. It is indeed a most awe inspiring place.

INDEX

PICTURE CREDITS